I0605920
UNITED STATES AIR FORCE
USAF
THUNDERBIRDS
UNITED STATES AIR FORCE
USAF

The Thunderbirds are the official U.S. Air Force air display team.

THUNDERBIRDS

HIGH FLYERS

CAROLINE "BLAZE" JENSEN

CREATIVE EDUCATION · CREATIVE PAPERBACKS

Published by Creative Education and Creative Paperbacks
P.O. Box 227, Mankato, Minnesota 56002
Creative Education and Creative Paperbacks are imprints of The Creative Company
www.thecreativecompany.us

Book Design by Tom Morgan
Art direction by Blue Design (www.bluedes.com)

Images by Pexels/Joseph Walker, 18, MICHAEL MCGARRY, 1, 16; Public Domain/11; U.S. Air Force/Staff Sgt. Bennie J. Davis III, 32, Tech. Sgt. Justin D. Pyle, 25, 31, Tech. Sgt. Matt Hecht, 22, Tech. Sgt. Sean M. White, 6; Unsplash/Aral Tasher, 20, Colin Lloyd, 2, Heber Davis, cover, 8, 28; Wikimedia Commons/Bill Stepehnson, USAF, 14, Duane Lempke, 27, Staff Sgt. Dakota Carter/U.S. Air Force, 4–5, 12–13, US Air Force, 7, 10

Library of Congress Cataloging-in-Publication Data
Names: Jensen, Caroline, author.
Title: Thunderbirds / Caroline "Blaze" Jensen.
Description: Mankato, Minnesota : Creative Education and Creative Paperbacks, [2026] | Series: High flyers | Includes bibliographical references and index. | Audience: Ages 10-13 | Audience: Grades 4-6 | Summary: "Diamond. Delta. High bomb burst. Author Caroline "Blaze" Jensen, former U.S. Air Force Thunderbirds fighter pilot, describes the elite skill it takes to perform stunning aerobatic displays. Soar high with the T-birds in this elegantly designed, visually stunning introduction to their history, present, and future, geared toward upper-elementary readers"— Provided by publisher.
Identifiers: LCCN 2025015381 (print) | LCCN 2025015382 (ebook) | ISBN 9798895810675 (library binding) | ISBN 9798896800200 (paperback) | ISBN 9798895811931 (ebook)
Subjects: LCSH: United States. Air Force. Thunderbirds--Juvenile literature. | Stunt flying—United States—Juvenile literature. | Aeronautics, Military—United States—Juvenile literature. | Air shows—United States—Juvenile literature. | CYAC: Stunt flying. | Military aeronautics. | Air shows.
Classification: LCC UG632.3.U6 J46 2026 (print) | LCC UG632.3.U6 (ebook) | DDC 797.5/40973—dc23/eng/20250512
LC record available at https://lccn.loc.gov/2025015381
LC ebook record available at https://lccn.loc.gov/2025015382

Printed in the United States

ABOUT THE AUTHOR — Caroline "Blaze" Jensen is an actual Thunderbird! She flew 3,600 hours in the Air Force as a fighter pilot, including F-16 combat missions and Thunderbirds demonstrations. She lives in Wisconsin with her son, Finn, and dog, Gunner. She loves sharing her passion for flying with kids of all ages.

The Thunderbirds team is made up of highly skilled pilots.

CONTENTS

WING TIPS

The F-16 fighter jets flown by the Thunderbirds are painted red, white, and blue. ↖

HIGH FLYERS

Meet the Thunderbirds

On May 15, 2006, the Thunderbirds, the United States Air Force Air Demonstration Squadron, flew over the crowd at Robins Air Force Base in Georgia. The fans cheered loudly. The pilots then performed their 4,000th show. The planes flew just 18 inches (45.7 centimeters) apart. The amazing loops, rolls, and formations showed what the F-16 fighter jet can do. These maneuvers were not just for show. The skilled pilots had thousands of hours of flight time combined. The red, white, and blue F-16s

A Republic F-84G Thunderjet 51-16719, flown by the Thunderbirds in 1954

could be equipped with ammunition and bombs within 72 hours to protect the country in a crisis.

Led by their commander, Lieutenant Colonel Kevin Robbins, the team was performing 70 airshows in 35 states throughout the year. The pilots, support officers, and maintenance team proudly represented the U.S. Air Force.

FROM STARDUSTERS TO THUNDERBIRDS

The team was first called the Stardusters but chose a stronger name. Its name, "Thunderbirds," comes from a huge mythical creature that controls the skies. Native Americans believe the Thunderbird can control the weather. The giant spirit bird creates thunder by flapping its wings and has lightning coming from its eyes. Just like the U.S. Air Force fighter jets protect U.S. combat forces, the Thunderbird is seen as a protector of Native Americans.

PATTILLO BROTHERS

The first Thunderbird wingmen were twin brothers. Bill Pattillo (below right) flew as right wing, and Charles "Buck" Pattillo (below left) flew as left wing. Bill was shot down during World War II (1939–45) and became a prisoner of war (POW) in Germany. Both brothers were combat veterans of World War II, the Korean War (1950–53), and the Vietnam War (1955–75). They retired as generals.

USAF
Thunderbirds
UNITED STATES AIR FORCE

The Thunderbirds soar high above the earth.

The Thunderbirds line up in perfect formations in the sky.

Fighter Jets and Fighter Pilots

The Thunderbirds have six demonstration pilots. Four pilots fly in a Diamond formation (commander/leader, right wing, left wing, and slot pilot), and two fly as solo pilots (lead solo and opposing solo). The team also has two additional pilots (the narrator and the director of operations), four support officers, and a crew of more than 120 enlisted airmen. Officers are college graduates who lead others and plan missions. Enlisted airmen do important hands-on work and usually start

their careers after high school or some college. They are experts in their fields and support the officers' decisions.

The Thunderbirds' mission is to show the capabilities of the high-performance jets during their hour-long show. The Thunderbirds began in 1953. At that time, the country was still learning about the new role of the U.S. Air Force, which had separated from the Army in 1947. The Thunderbirds were created to show the power of a new jet that would be flown in the Korean War, demonstrate what combat fighter pilots could do, and recruit new pilots to the Air Force.

FIRST SUPERSONIC JET DEMONSTRATION

The F-105 Thunderchief was one of the Air Force's first supersonic fighter jets. Supersonic means faster than the speed of sound, which is about 776 miles (1,234.4 kilometers) per hour. When a jet goes faster than the speed of sound, it breaks the sound barrier and makes a sonic boom because it catches up to the sound waves. The F-105 was replaced by other aircraft but remains a milestone for the Air Force and the Thunderbirds.

The Korean War was fought from 1950 to 1953. During this war, the F-84G Thunderjet was one of the main fighters used in combat. The first Thunderbirds team had five F-84Gs. Major General Dick Catledge was the first commander/leader of the Thunderbirds. The Thunderbirds became a squadron on May 25, 1953. They had just three weeks to prepare for their first air demonstration, which took place on July 1, 1953, at Luke Air Force Base in Phoenix, Arizona.

The Thunderbirds have flown seven different aircraft in their history. After the F-86G Thunderjet and the F-84F Thunderstreak, they flew the world's first supersonic fighter, the F-100 Super Sabre. They also flew the Republic F-105 Thunderchief, the F-4E Phantom, and the T-38 Talon, the world's first supersonic jet trainer.

In 1982, the four Diamond pilots crashed simultaneously in their T-38s during a practice in Nevada. After the terrible accident, it seemed like the Thunderbirds would be grounded forever. But General W. L. "Bill" Creech, who had flown with the Thunderbirds soon after they began, convinced members of Congress that the team was an important recruiting tool. The Thunderbirds were allowed to keep flying. The team started to fly again in the new, more powerful and maneuverable F-16 Fighting Falcon.

All Thunderbird team members are incredibly talented and special. Some made history by being part of the team. One is General Lloyd "Fig" Newton, the first African American man to fly with the Thunderbirds. General Newton was the narrator, right wing, and slot pilot. Colonel Nicole "Fifi" Malachowski was the first woman pilot on the demonstration squadron. She flew as the right wing.

CALLSIGNS

Air Force fighter pilots have special callsigns, which are nicknames given to them when they join a fighter squadron. Pilots use callsigns when they talk to each other. These names are based on their names, personality, or something funny that happened to them. For example, someone who accidentally went supersonic and broke some windows might be called "Boomer." Someone who accidentally set a field on fire by dropping a flare might be called "Smokey." What would your callsign be?

HIGH FLYERS

How to Become a Thunderbird

Many people dream of flying airplanes, and for those who love airplanes, becoming a pilot on the Thunderbirds is a huge dream. The Thunderbird team is more than six pilots flying jets in precision formations at airshows. There are more than 130 Air Force members who do 25 different jobs to help the team travel. They handle everything from travel arrangements to writing stories, taking photographs, and maintaining the F-16s. The

Thunderbird pilots are chosen from the best in the Air Force.

people selected for these roles are some of the best in their careers before they join the Thunderbirds.

To become a Thunderbird pilot, you must graduate from college. You can attend colleges with a Reserve Officer Training Corps (ROTC) program or go to the United States Air Force Academy (USAFA) in Colorado Springs, Colorado. You need good grades in school. You may become an officer through ROTC, USAFA, or Officer Training School (OTS) and compete for pilot training. Pilots must pass training and physical exams. Eventually, any future Thunderbird must become an Air Force fighter pilot.

Pilots train on small, specialized jets. They learn combat skills and how to handle stressful situations. They learn to be part of a bigger team, even though they are in one small airplane. Fighter pilots must be skilled at doing many things at the same time. They must talk on two different radios, look out for threats from the ground and the air, make sure they don't run out of fuel, and know where the other jets are, all while flying their own plane. After flying for a few years and gaining experience in a fighter aircraft, a pilot can apply to fly with the Thunderbirds. Each step of this process is very competitive.

Once a pilot qualifies, they begin a long application process. Pilots send in flying records to be reviewed. They have letters from their leaders recommending

them for their pilot skills, leadership skills, and dedication to representing the best of the Air Force. They must write a letter explaining why they want to be a Thunderbird pilot and send a photo in their uniform. A select few applicants will be chosen to join the Thunderbirds for an airshow where they will learn about all the jobs on the team, how the team operates, and how it interacts with the community. Thunderbird pilots and their enlisted teammates visit schools and speak to students to encourage them to follow their dreams. They also visit hospitals and sick children and spend time with community leaders at each airshow location. The pilots are carefully interviewed, and only the best of the best are offered the opportunity to join the team.

UNITED STATES AIR FORCE ACADEMY GRADUATION

The Thunderbirds are a special part of the United States Air Force Academy graduation. At the end of the graduation ceremony, a high-ranking general says, "Class of (insert year), YOU ARE DISMISSED," and the six Thunderbirds roar overhead in a Delta formation as the white caps fly in the air. Everyone cheers because it is the end of four years of hard work and the beginning of a career in the U.S. Air Force. The sound and sight of the jets flying low and fast, in perfect formation, make the special moment even more exciting and memorable for everyone.

An airman conducts an early morning walk-around of an F-16 Thunderbird Fighting Falcon

Training for a Safe Show

The home of the Thunderbirds is Nellis Air Force Base in Las Vegas, Nevada. The pilots train from Las Vegas, but they've also flown in El Centro and Edwards Air Force Base, California, during the training season. They usually fly twice every day. The pilots train to be either part of the Diamond formation or one of the solos. The Diamond is made of the commander/leader, right wing, left wing, and slot pilots. The commander/leader is the number 1 jet, also called "the Boss." The number 2 pilot is the left wing, and the number 3 pilot is the right wing. The wing pilots often

When the Thunderbirds start training, they fly at higher altitudes and just in twos. They practice easier maneuvers at first.

mirror each other from opposite sides of the Diamond. The slot pilot, or number 4, flies directly behind the Boss's jet and lower and behind the wingmen. The Diamond performs precision maneuvers like loops and rolls while maintaining tight formation positions. Thunderbirds number 5 and number 6 are the solo pilots. They show the power and maneuverability of the F-16. They perform high-speed passes. Thunderbird number 5 often flies upside down, which is why the 5 on the side of their jet is printed upside down. It looks right side up when passing in front of the crowd.

hen the Thunderbirds start training, they fly at higher altitudes and just in twos. They practice easier maneuvers at first, then gradually work toward more difficult maneuvers. They add more jets and get closer to the ground. They practice until they can perform their stunts safely. This is important because flying for the Thunderbirds can be very dangerous.

Twenty-one Thunderbirds have died while performing their duties for the team. One of the worst crashes was on January 18, 1982, when four Diamond

Thunderbird pilots are experts at flying very close safely.

pilots crashed during practice north of Nellis Air Force Base. The Diamond was practicing a loop maneuver. The leader did not make the 100-foot (30.5-meter) clearance from the ground, and all four aircraft crashed in perfect formation. There were no survivors. A painting of the four pilots—Major Norm Lowry, III, commander/leader; Captain Willie Mays, left wing; Captain Joseph "Pete" Peterson, right wing; and Captain Mark E. Melancon, slot pilot—hangs in the Thunderbirds' hangar. This is so the team will never forget the sacrifice of those who gave their lives for the important mission of the Thunderbirds. The best way to honor those who died doing what they loved is to keep doing it and learn from the mistakes to make it a safer and better show.

ne memorable moment for all flying and non-flying members is when they get to wear the Thunderbird patch. This means they are an essential member of a very important team. When the pilots complete their training, they get something special that only Thunderbird pilots get to wear: a shiny helmet. The helmet is red in the front and white, with blue stars and the patch, in the back. Just like the jets, it represents the colors of the United States. A lot of hard work goes into earning the right to wear the patch and helmet, despite the danger.

THE AIR FORCE MEMORIAL

The Air Force Memorial (pictured below) at Arlington National Cemetery in Virginia represents three jets climbing skyward, as in the Thunderbird High Bomb Burst. One jet is missing, representing those who were lost. It is also called "the Missing Man Formation" and honors those who served.

The Thunderbirds have never canceled a show because they were not ready to fly.

The Air Demonstration

The Thunderbirds fly about 30 shows and are on the road for around 250 days each year. They have performed in all 50 states and 58 foreign countries. A large panel of flags on the sides of the jets shows all the countries where they have performed.

The Thunderbirds have never had to cancel a show due to maintenance or because the jets were not ready to fly. If one of the jets has a maintenance problem, another jet is ready for them to switch to, so they can continue the show.

The ground crew has their own show at most sites. They show their precision in getting the pilots into the aircraft and starting the aircraft safely. Ground crew members walk around and talk to the audience. They are on the radio, talking to the pilots throughout the show to tell them how well they are meeting the timing and maneuver goals. Someone is even in charge of making sure the music matches the maneuvers perfectly, like an airshow DJ.

The best time to fly is when the wind is light and the sky is clear. The main show is when the clouds are high enough to do the loop and roll maneuvers. However, the team is prepared for when the weather isn't perfectly clear. If the clouds are lower, the Thunderbirds perform a version of the show with the same maneuvers, but they aren't as high. If the weather is bad, they can perform a "flat show." The team flies at 500 feet (152.4 meters) or less, so they do no loops and no rolls.

The F-16s are modified with a smoke system that sprays smoke oil into the exhaust near the afterburner—the section near the back of the plane where flames show. The temperature of the exhaust turns the oil into bright white smoke that trails behind the jets. The smoke is important for safety. It helps the pilots see each other during maneuvers and helps the audience see the maneuvers. But the tricky pilots don't always want to be seen right away.

One of the crowd's favorite maneuvers is the Sneak Pass. As the crowd watches the Diamond flying a difficult maneuver in front of them, one of the solos sneaks up from behind the crowd and flies over their heads low and as fast as possible without going supersonic. The crowd is startled, and then they laugh at how amazing it was to have a jet fly over so low and fast!

Bright white smoke helps the pilots see each other.

One of the most recognized maneuvers is the High Bomb Burst. The four Diamond pilots pull straight up at the sky in perfect formation. The Boss directs them all to turn their smoke on and roll quickly to fly off in four different directions. They fly away from each other for a few miles and, on the Boss's command, dive down towards the earth. They face each other to pass with their noses pointing at one another and cross over a point at the same time. The crowd gasps! It looks like the planes might all hit! But they pass one another and immediately maneuver to rejoin safely.

The Thunderbirds are not just about flying. They show audiences what is possible when people work together and love what they do. They continue to inspire audiences everywhere, showing that practice and teamwork make the U.S. Air Force one of the best in the world.

INDEX